The Mercy of Night

First published in the UK by Beacon Books and Media Ltd
Earl Business Centre, Dowry Street, Oldham, OL8 2PF, UK.

www.beaconbooks.net

Cataloging-in-Publication record for this book is available from the
British Library

ISBN 978-1-916955-74-5 Paperback
ISBN 978-1-916955-75-2 Hardback

Cover image: Antonio Jose Soriano – stock.adobe.com

The Mercy of Night

Lutfi Al-Nufoury

BB
BEACON BOOKS

Foreword

Sometimes, holding on to poetic patterns, prosody and rules ruins the poetic experience and renders emotional outpourings tasteless. It is beneficial, rather sweet, to let the wild, raw yet innocent, untainted and untampered human feelings find their way out into this wilderness, without trying to intervene with versification or classification.

In that, strange sounds can be heard; these are sounds of agony mixed with regret, crying mixed with smiles, only if smiles can have a sound. (It is quite interesting that smiling has no sound, as if the happiest moments of human beings are the silentness.) It is this mixture of feelings called 'human being' that represents the riddle that Allah has deposited in the human self to open the door to life-long exploration.

إِنَّا خَلَقْنَا ٱلْإِنسَـٰنَ مِن نُّطْفَةٍ أَمْشَاجٍ نَّبْتَلِيهِ فَجَعَلْنَـٰهُ سَمِيعًا بَصِيرًا ٢

We created man from a drop of mingled fluid to put him to the test; We gave him hearing and sight. (76:2)

These poems delve into the depths of those meanings and feelings. They are raw and truthful, loud and silent, speaking to the soul and invoking reflection. In all of that, they don't abide by rules of courtesy called rhyme and rhythm, because they just transcribe heartbeats as they come. I have found them no more enjoyable than profound and I have conversed with them intellectually and emotionally at every turn of reading, or rather traversing through their routes. I pray that Lutfi's pen never dries.

Ahmed Saad Al-Azhari
7th November 2024

Preface

Whilst he does not enter into all of these poems, my father's memory was certainly the mountain in the background as I wrote them, as solid as he was in life. And I do not mean to paint death as a tragedy beyond all proportion. There are things worse than death, more violent and more fierce. I know that many of us are facing formidable trials, day in and day out, struggling in ways both obvious and imperceptibly subtle. Nevertheless, when you lose somebody so close to you the complaints of your heart become deafening.

In the early days the clamour drowns out your sense completely. And, although the mind may try to exert control, there will be times when it is naturally overrun. But with this overrunning a wonderful kind of truth emerges, and a unique tranquillity. Not euphoria of course, but a stony solidity, and a necessary reordering of reality.

With Allah as my witness I would not trade my life for any other. And if this book brings true benefit to anyone then I will be very happy.

Dr. Lutfi Al-Nufoury
22nd Sha'ban 1445/ 3rd March 2024

For my father,

Dr. Maysan Al-Nufoury

1381–1445 AH

وَجَعَلْنَا نَوْمَكُمْ سُبَاتًا

And We made your sleep for rest

وَجَعَلْنَا ٱلَّيْلَ لِبَاسًا

And We made the night as a cover

(78:9–10)

بِسْمِ اللَّهِ الرَّحْمَنِ الرَّحِيمِ

1.

without Your Mercy
there would be no open gardens
on this earth for us to delight in

hold on, let me begin again

without Your mercy
our hearts would be ships
wrecked against jagged cliffs

hold on, let me begin again

without Your mercy
we would be extinct, hunted
by the Jinn or by our own selves

hold on, let me begin again

without Your mercy
I would never even
have picked up this pen

hold on
please
let me begin again

2.

prayers in perfect harmony
dressed beautifully
with openings aplenty
and the fragrance
flowing through the chosen few
are these the dearer
or the prayers of holding on
clothes spoiled by day
mind toiling, fibrillating
tawhīd is our only chance
so incomplete, and dragging feet
we put ourselves in mercy's way
before I start I say
be gone, Iblīs

3.

onyx sleep
deep sea diving sleep
mountains of pasta and cheese
sinking, sinking sleep
each red blood cell shouting bye bye
to my body
that's how I join the current,
pulled as if I were a
maltreated alley cat
manhandled by my tail
navigating the winding
ocean backstreets
that's how I join the current of sleep
huge waves, slow and heavenly
shimmering vault over me
and I hear the thundering
distant feet of an army
marching over crayons
and plastic beakers
and apricot hills
like that, my body joins the current
and my soul goes wherever it goes

4.

someone said it's like losing
the roof over your head

now here I lie, exposed to biting gales
I never knew existed

and someone else said
whilst we sat, at the beginning

of our grief
was that your dad's seat?

but every seat was Dad's seat

5.

pull me up to the halls of my dreams,
what a strange command

that's what I say to myself at sleep's door.
I lock the car and throw away the key

the fire's on its way home, or it should
be anyway. I made sure those hungry

ashes had access to air—they crave it but it
burns them right out.

I am so tired of those nuances
that would serve to part

a muslim from a muslim
so let Allah draw distinctions now

and sort through the differences later on.
And a cell may only differentiate

when the time is right—when He ordains,
for good or bad. What a beautiful night,

Victorian brown. Sherlock Holmes steps out
on nights like this, strolling

smoking his pipe—the smoke rings are blue
and by the way, I mean the old

Sherlock Holmes, not the new.
And know this—understanding desire

is more satisfying than the desire itself.
And waking up is naught but changing

from a state of powerlessness
to a state of power.

And whatever God bestows
will always remain as His to take

6.

having spent my entire life in their service, picking my silent steps between them for days on end, and having slept so many nights here nestled in my cot (that must surely be the only space for a living soul for many miles)—I have come to accept the idea that each grave is its own universe.

It may seem a strange thing for me to say, since I have no qualifications other than tending to the dead and their housing, and I am certainly no great thinker by anyone's measure. But I believe it, and I cannot but help feel it again as I stand over yet another fresh plot, the dust overlying it being a very pleasing brown (the colour of milky coffee, though it's hard to say exactly, since I last had a coffee several years ago).

I dug and flattened this one only yesterday, but now there is no sign of my effort or sweat anywhere to be seen

7.

the dusk came down fast—in part brutally,
as a hammer blow, and in part as a mercy

like an old friend's hand across my back.
And when I drive like this

in this mood, I mean, I am almost bionic
ballistic of heart and quite cold

melded to red lights ahead and beyond,
and to all of the drivers of all of the cars

like so, we sit in the glow, like so many
delegates at the conference of night.

Yes, these are the days in which fierce
analysis fails.

A white van cuts in, I'm annoyed and then
pleased. I've always needed a guide

and it seems he knows the way tonight
so he drives and I write

***

I wonder if birds are still flying with the same
exquisite reverence around the mosque

of the Umayyads. Let's go, I said. SubhanAllah,
and the reason came. Sunni, Shia, I stick

to my stance and yet admit—we probably follow
our parents in it. Gone are the Ād, Thamūd,

the Madyan, and the people of Lūt—a curse upon
their houses. Out here we long for the quiet

embrace of courtyards and the avuncular
company of old wooden doors

in the Islamic style, of course. In the Islamic
style, we while away the hours, minds tiled

like Nūr al-Dīn's bathhouse. Steam
clouds the entrances and exits. Far away

from the wrought iron tricks of modern life
and wave upon wave of coryzal symptoms.

And forever, I reject that blind momentum.
I wonder if birds still fly with the same

reverence around that ancient gold, and over
worshippers below. Those tired, hurt

but constantly refilling their hearts
with the succour of their Lord

like battered brass vessels, those that are
lifted each day to take on pure water.

And the way to live is to make yourself an
army, marching on and on through spring,

armour glowing, still caught up in the romance
of it all, before the first man falls

8.

I am still learning this language
but in burning heat
the letters melt so easily

I once misread the poem
written on a dusty coffee cup
it said everything is beautiful

in one way or another
but I read
all roads to you are beautiful

9.

seventeen trees, cut-card against night
only souls see souls in this new wasteland
and I put the rest of the dunya
into storage.
These seventeen trees
are cut-card against night,
I can't be bothered sometimes
I begin to speak and then stop.
Because needless expression is
bracing at first—like the vigour and power
of red-coated armies
leading me on to the deadest of ends

10.

hold this, Abī, and so
I hold on to my dad's blood
flowing in and out
in an eerie tidal sweep

whirring clicking white machine
it beeps as if to soothe me
lovely and melodic
he couldn't live without it

we talk about blood pressure
his input and his output
we hide behind my stethoscope
we slip into a dream

where we are young and strong
and we sit atop the plain
the grasses sway and murmur
and nobody needs doctors anymore

11.

love is not a helpless state

12.

solitude is sweet when it's
for a purpose

so is this rain
and this traffic jam
and this piece of toast

I smile at the Roman cement
of loving you
and the Prophet ﷺ

if he said it or did it
it is good

13.

barzakh (Arabic): partition/barrier

I lie down with your voice
in my head
I sink into the sheets
Lo
something this way comes!

(is it better for a stone to skim
ten times, or just to do one big one,
ten miles long?)
I sink into the sheets
Lo, something this way comes!

my line is on my mind
I am worried it will fade
so I made a simple coat of arms
from silver, gold and green
I sink into the sheets

like a smoothened stone,
unskimmed
and when nothing comes at all
that's how I know
I'm at the barzakh

where death
is a kind of sleep,
is a kind of death,
is a kind of sleep,
is a kind of death

14.

if my life was a street
of parallel parked memories
lined with cosy terraces

my love for you would not be found
in autumn trees, or in the lovely
subtleties of poetry

my love would be a fire engine
sirens blaring
waking everyone up

15.

what about that violent change
chasing the endless loose
threads of your culture
woven or unwoven, worn or new
such a person seems to hold sway over you
and she wears this, and he bends the truth
just like that
my favourite restaurant is closing
what do you think about this new language
I have decided to cherish
what about pain
what about pain
what about the feeling the Shaytān has
unchained in you
and what about those cattle in pairs
and those rituals forbidden
or that song that means so much to you today
you soon got sick of
and what about the light reflecting
off the farrier's blade
he stands admiring his own handiwork
a millennium later it's gone
the creases of his palm are empty
and the horse is dead

Thomas Hardy once wrote
of a shepherd whose head hit the pillow
and he slept, quicker than it takes you or I
to even get comfortable
so don't even try to get comfortable here

16.

panda lion elephant
leopard kitty cat
you loved them more than anything
your smile could cut the sky in half

17.

my brief notes
my grief notes
the lies that give me brief hope
but then I know, it's not so wise
to force a rhyme, where there is none
I float across the car park
this is easy
one-foot, two-foot, masjid door
if it were guarded by a mountain lion
I wouldn't know
I wouldn't care
and through the prayer I dip
into sujūd, as if my head were sinking
it's the weight
of this unwanted crown
a son's succession, it's not grand
it's naught but tears for you
and overflowing love
and what I have of
grief, I give

18.

and just like that he called out to his maid,
barked to his faithful maid, an old woman
who had served them long and long. Naturally
(without a look), she was well aware of every
nook and cranny of the house, of every
happening and quiet spot—she felt it all.
Diligently, with strong and supple hands,
she threw a cot onto the floor for the traveller,
a rough linen mat, stuffed well with warm
fuzz. And then two soft synthetic blankets,
broad and long to wrap his body in, comforting
his limbs. There he would lie and sleep awhile,
patterned in the warm browns and swirling
creams of this temporary bed. He would find a
type of momentary comfort there, she
thought.

As if my own son, I'll treat him as my
own flesh and blood. And finally, she took two
fresh and heavy pillows for his young and
troubled head—she laid them down. She put
them down with care and there he slept, dead
to the world—spilling out his dreams onto the
whiteness, just as dark blood, flowing,
leaves a split skull

19.

insulated, like an ostrich egg
I sit back, hands behind my head

and these couplets are my daily bread
there's no money it

only fathomless freedom of mind. And I
always loved the description

of Achilles as the matchless runner—
nothing to bind him

because in my mind, the desert is endless,
and it makes my blood boil

in a good way. One day, one day.
One day, when I saw that

I was nothing, I chose to put myself in a cage.
A gentle one, a great one,

born from a warm night breeze,
creeping like a happy skeleton

or from the du'a of an ancestor, better than me
and more likely to be accepted.

So do what I did. Stop, now, and recite
the Qur'an

let it stitch the rags of your life together
with golden thread. It is beauty you can't draw

you can only draw it out.
And when I saw my faults crystallised,

I cried, and I asked my teacher,
and he said that's how it is

because they are all real
and because knowing is the first step

20.

because knowing is the first step. And I miss all the
sins I could have prevented

and I miss heaven, though I have never seen it
and I wish I could have cleansed

the world, or cooked a meal for my living
father, kissing his forehead

not from love, but from pure respect.
Listen again—there is nothing more beautiful

in this world than the way the sun catches
a battered air-conditioning vent

and cotton shirts, drying on the backs of plastic
chairs. Not in and of themselves,

but each as a symbol of pure inner peace
and tranquillity

these come from Allah only
if you don't know that yet, it's ok, go back

to the beginning, take a deep breath,
set your compass to Him, you will not fail

21.

like the last image in the world
a man in an ill-fitting suit jacket
pads through a metal detector
in his socks

that jacket is probably not Prada
but Prada isn't everything
he's going to Vienna or Berlin
and the whole scene makes

me wish that electricity
had never actually been born
do you ever feel like that?
Ok, I'll carry on then

the second to last image
in the world is scrubland
viewed from train windows
ringed with dust

what remains of the horizon
is bare and folded over
like a reused envelope
and dry winds

rattle sweet and hollow
like the breath of a fasting believer.
Here your loved one sits next
to you, although you haven't

met her yet. You reach out a hand
to touch a future
only God can provide
for He is The Provider

and The Sustainer
and you yourself
cannot arrive at a single atom
without His leave.

Now I return to my somewhat
weakened descriptions
can you guess what's next?
the man got stopped

and ordered to take off his
suit jacket
it turns out it was Prada after all
but the cut was drastically wrong

22.

the last lavender
dances with a bumble bee
they both look knackered

23.

there were days of strength
like when I washed and buried you
with my own hands

and there were days of weakness
where I left the city of my mind
and camped on the outskirts

24.

I'll never stop trying to find the one I love
silently underscoring, my words ash on this breeze
but wrapping me up heavy

that's the lament of travelling for you
I will navigate bland highways forever, if needs be
and hearts accept both petrol and diesel

so don't worry, they won't stop.
I am written as a parent to my children eternally
and my parents to me, so death will be nothing

between us. And if you feel security in me whilst
I'm open to the elements then fine
I'll make a good tent, cuddly toy or hat

and that would be a better use for me.
Yā bunayyatī! Let me build you a shop in the desert
where you can get your carrots and pasta

I'll carry you miles and miles to get there
I'll make you porridge, blow on it, to cool it down,
and then struggle with your travel cot

under scorching sun.
I was simple, ideas rippled,
then you punched me spiritually

and now I testify that a parent's love
for their child is not describable here.
But let me ask you,

by way of understanding what is dear
to the heart of a believer—
why was Sayyidina Ibrahim's act so great?

25.

there is no homeland
there is no phone line connecting
you to that which you seek
there are no hearty rocks
that long for your vigil
no part of earth is waiting
for your big symbolic kiss
though you may think all this

and I once felt at home
when I heard the Adhān
and the row in front of me opened
and the next
and the next
and the next
and the next
and onwards I stepped

26.

the matter is complicated
and the matter will always be complicated

but the matter is also a simple one
and that's not poetic licence

it's demonstrable, logical
probable and reasonable

like how the nighttime jaguar
will always be grey

with eyes like molten silver
and rosettes that slip away

then reappear like undiscovered
particulate matter

and yet, the daytime jaguar is
snarling and proud

a lazy soldier
its markings deep and vivid

with golden syrup fur
singed by close encounter.

True—on their rare, refined campaigns
these two cats are the same

but the nighttime jaguar growls
the louder.

I am far from the meridian
but driving on with purpose untold

and the nighttime jaguar growls
the louder

and without light, the prevailing
state is night

and the nighttime jaguar growls
the louder

and I don't get cold, and I never give up
and I ask only from God

and the nighttime jaguar growls
the louder

27.

love is not a helpless state, naturally. I don't
call myself a Sufi or Salafi any more than I call
myself a Montague or Capulet
love is not a helpless state, that word is
marred, twisted into an empty order. The word
love is in pain
it should be treated better
we should learn about our own souls first
and then, and only then
we can return to love again

28.

I remember that first night, I took not
a second of sleep and arose
neck stiff and twisted like an anchor

and even that was a mercy, a sign
to show me how much I loved you.
And still love you, since your soul still

exists, revelling in the good to come
InshaAllah.
What a beautiful thing, when the curtains

are drawn on a life. We seek refuge
in Allah, and we seek refuge in His night.
And so again, I return like a tide

under the blankets, to take in
my strength. No food, no water
just sleep

Appendix: dream fragments

one more step

*I have reached the point where I no longer look younger
than my age
I think my eyes give it away
people will say it's my grey hair*

*and walking stick
my stoop and grizzly chin but I think it's my eyes*

with a ruler and protractor, I measure the sky's wingspan

that cloud, over there, is a massive grey whale

*there was a time when Allah's punishment hurtled to-
wards cities*

*everything is easy for Him. He allows me to doze in peace
on my forefather's lands*

*and my arrogance is a comfortable bed yet I know that
being cut down to size*

*is a cure for almost all ills
and that in brokenness there is light*

*and in demolition there is freedom. We are sorry it had to
be this way, sir
it's ok. When I am having a rough day, or month or year,
I smile inside
and my heart becomes hollower, and much happier*

it can be inconvenient
for example, honestly
there's too much granite in this kitchen

don't fret for a second on identity, you are wasted there.
You came from so many nice lines, split across so many
memories

but all good, like taking a knife
to a bowl of fruit. You must mark out what's best and
carve out
your meaning through deeds.
no labels please, don't sit wondering, hugged by the light
of lying screens
stand up please, you can do better. You are a Muslim, you
travelled far for this
you can do better

you don't need to wait for someone to say I love you too

you already have everything

endless ground covered
in holy sanctuary
where wide searing days
give way to gorgeous evening, nestled in the valley
volcanic rocks pen in
the weighty city

the gracious city
the pilgrims whirl

the pilgrims whirl

forever it seems, amassed, a white galaxy wrapped
around gravity's

sharp black corners

catching glimpses of gold
this is the home of secret secrets

and open majesty
and maybe ritual is the hardest

thing to grasp
but it cuts the deepest

so take me back

by the road where the lone camel grazes

count all of his ribs and imagine his thirst

under fell sun that never forgives and

be grateful